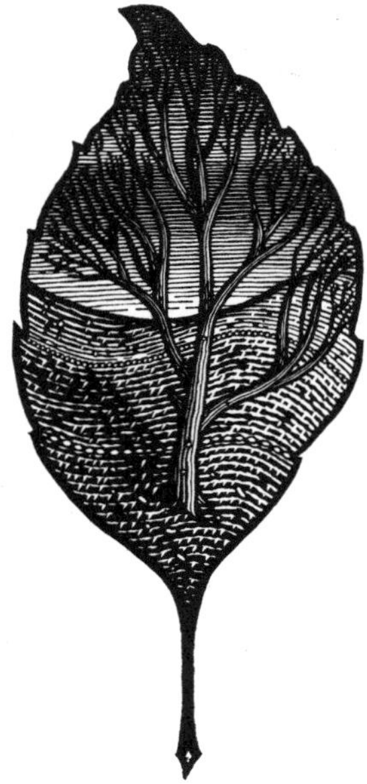

from **The Heart of the Tree**

Henry Cuyler Bunner (1855-1896)

What does he plant who plants a tree?
He plants the friend of sun and sky;
He plants the flag of breezes free;
The shaft of beauty, towering high;
He plants a home to heaven anigh
For song and mother-croon of bird
In hushed and happy twilight heard –
The treble of heaven's harmony –
These things he plants who plants a tree.

Treelines

A collection of poems

LAUTUS PRESS

Also published by Lautus Press

Washing Lines: A collection of poems
Strings of Pearls: A collection of poems
Shorelines: A collection of poems
all selected by Janie Hextall and Barbara McNaught

This collection was first published 2018
Lautus Press, Ryton House, Lechlade, GL7 3AR

ISBN: 978-0-9568265-3-4

© Janie Hextall and Barbara McNaught 2018

Designed and typeset in Minion Pro and Johnston
by Neil Morgan Design, Cheltenham
Printed by Holywell Press, Oxford

A CIP catalogue record for this book is available from the British Library

Contents

Henry Cuyler Bunner *The Heart of the Tree*	Frontispiece
Wendell Berry *Look it Over*	8
Michael S Glaser *A Blessing for the Woods*	9
Alice Oswald *Woods etc.*	10
John Clare *Pleasant Sounds*	11
Sue Butler *Trees*	12
Esther Morgan *Planting* from *Labours*	13
Michael Longley *Hazel*	14
Seamus Heaney *Planting the Alder*	15
Alice Oswald *Leaf for J.O. and L.O.*	16
Philip Larkin *The Trees*	17
Charlotte Brontë *The Wood*	18
Alice Oswald *Wood Not Yet Out*	19
Jon Stallworthy *Windfalls*	20
A E Housman *Loveliest of Trees*	21
Sydney Matthewman *Orchard Idyll*	22
Kerry Hardie *May Rain*	23
Fleur Adcock *Trees*	24
Jane Hirshfield *Tree*	26
Elizabeth Bishop *To a Tree*	27
Clive James *Winter Plums*	28
Gillian Clarke *Wild Plums*	29
Ruth Gilbert *Into the Trees*	30
D H Lawrence *Trees in the Garden*	31
Ilo Orleans *The Shadow Tree*	32
Paul Batchelor *Tree Climbing*	33
Helen Dunmore *The plum tree*	34
Jane Kenyon *Coming Home at Twilight in Late Summer*	35
Helen Dunmore *A mortgage on a pear tree*	36
Eavan Boland *Daphne with her Thighs in Bark*	38
John Clare *The Shepherd's Tree*	40
Michael Longley *The Beech Tree*	41

Gillian Clarke *The Oak Wood*	42
Robert Graves *Not Dead*	43
Carol Ann Duffy *The English Elms*	44
Adrienne Rich *What Kind of Times are These*	46
Don Paterson *Two Trees*	47
Wendell Berry *The Sycamore*	48
John Clare *The Hollow Tree*	49
Harriet Fraser *Wealth in Difference*	50
Rudyard Kipling *The Way through the Woods*	51
Jim Carruth *Lawmarnock Wood in Autumn*	52
Rainer Maria Rilke *The Apple Orchard*	54
Alison Brackenbury *Apple Country*	55
Kerry Hardie *Leaf-fall*	56
Choman Hardi *Leaves*	57
Paul Farley *Whitebeam*	58
C S Lewis *The Future of Forestry*	59
Seamus Heaney *The Poplar*	60
Gerard Manley Hopkins *Binsey Poplars*	61
Ruth Gilbert *Given: A Log of Wood; Make: A Fiddle*	62
Anon *Prayer of the Woods*	63
William Carlos Williams *Winter Trees*	64
Richard Wilbur *A Black Birch in Winter*	65
Wendy Cope *Haiku: Willows*	66
Alice Oswald *Pruning in Frost*	67
James Joyce *In the Dark Pine-wood*	68
Rupert Brooke *Pine Trees and the Sky: Evening*	69
Ralph Waldo Emerson *See yonder leafless trees*	70
Ruth Fainlight *Those Trees*	71
e e cummings *little tree*	72
Wendy Cope *The Tree*	73
Celia Congreve *The Firewood Poem*	74
Roger McGough *Mr Pollard*	75
Matsuo Basho *The Oak Tree*	76
Mervyn Peake *With People, So With Trees*	77
Michael Shepherd *The Poet Tree*	79

Illustrations

Jonathan Ashworth *The Whole Tree*	Endpapers
Howard Phipps *Edge of the Woods*	8
Eric Ravilious from *Diary (1933)*	11
Clare Leighton *Warm Weather Coming*	12
Clare Leighton *Hazel Catkins*	14
Anne Hayward *Blackthorn Clouds – Tanglewood*	17
Sue Scullard *Apple Blossom*	20
Miriam Macgregor *When Birds do Sing*	22
Alexander Cozens *Quercus, oak*	25
Jonathan Gibbs *Tree at my Window*	27
George Nicholson *Plums* from *The Illustrated Dictionary of Gardening*	29
Tree climbing	32
Anita Klein *Goddess of the Pear Tree*	37
Illustration from *Eclogues* in *Vergilius Romanus* (5th century)	41
Sue Scullard *Steadfast Oaks*	43
Carry Akroyd *Elm*	45
Jacob George Strutt *Sir Philip Sidney's Oak*	49
Reynolds Stone	53
Clare Melinsky *Rosy Red Apples*	55
Joan Hassall *Gathered Leaves*	57
Lombardy Poplars	60
John F Greenwood *Nessfield Road*	64
Richard Wagener *Shuteye Peak Afternoon*	68
Kay Leverton *Dance of the Crows*	70
Carry Akroyd *December*	73
Jonathan Ashworth *Girls that Axe*	75
Howard Phipps *Downs in Winter*	76
Reynolds Stone	79

Look It Over
Wendell Berry

I leave behind even
my walking stick. My knife
is in my pocket, but that
I have forgot. I bring
no car, no cell phone,
no computer, no camera,
no CD player, no fax, no
TV, not even a book. I go
into the woods. I sit on
a log provided at no cost.
It is the earth I've come to,
the earth itself, sadly
abused by the stupidity
only humans are capable of
but, as ever, itself. Free.
A bargain! Get it while it lasts.

A Blessing for the Woods
Michael S Glaser

Before I leave, almost without noticing,
before I cross the road and head toward
what I have intentionally postponed –

Let me stop to say a blessing for these woods:
for crows barking and squirrels scampering,
for trees and fungus and multi-coloured leaves,

for the way sunlight laces shadows
through each branch and leaf of tree,
for these paths that take me in,
for these paths that lead me out.

Woods etc.
Alice Oswald

footfall, which is a means so steady
and in small sections wanders through the mind
unnoticed, because it beats constantly,
sweeping together the loose tacks of sound

I remember walking once into increasing
woods, my hearing like a widening wound.
first your voice and then the rustling ceasing.
the last glow of rain dead in the ground

that my feet kept time with the sun's imaginary
changing position, hoping it would rise
suddenly from scattered parts of my body
into the upturned apses of my eyes.

no clearing in that quiet, no change at all.
in my throat the little mercury line
that regulates my speech began to fall
rapidly the endless length of my spine

Pleasant Sounds
John Clare (1793-1864)

The rustling of leaves under the feet in woods and under
 hedges;
The crumpling of cat-ice and snow down wood-rides,
 narrow lanes and every street causeway;
Rustling through a wood or rather rushing, while the wind
 halloos in the oak-toop like thunder;
The rustle of birds' wings startled from their nests or flying
 unseen into the bushes;
The whizzing of larger birds overhead in a wood, such as
 crows, puddocks, buzzards;
The trample of robins and woodlarks on the brown leaves.
 and the patter of squirrels on the green moss;
The fall of an acorn on the ground, the pattering of nuts on
 the hazel branches as they fall from ripeness;
The flirt of the groundlark's wing from the stubbles –
 how sweet such pictures on dewy mornings, when the
dew flashes from its brown feathers.

Trees
Sue Butler

I cycle up the hill above your house,
sit on a gate to a stubble field.
Your spade shines in coastal sun
as you slice through your shadow
and turf, into rich black loam; ancient,
terrifying. A neat circle cut,
you dig down, sprinkle stardust from a bag.
You hold the sapling straight, backfill,
heel it in. A rainbow
pours from the watering can.
You wipe sweat from your face, look up.
I wave, but all you see is land
that could yield
apples pressed to cider, drunk
in shade. A man planting trees
isn't leaving his wife,
whatever you say. You're not leaving.

from **Labours**
Esther Morgan

1 *Planting*

Hawthorn, hazel, hornbeam –
the estate's old retainer

heels them, barely more than twigs,
like crosses into the light sandy soil –

native species deer and rabbit
would strip, come winter,

if it weren't for the spirals of plastic
he slots into place around each one.

So the autumn passes at the same unhurried pace
of a man who knows there's a long way to go,

who seems, by All Souls, to have been here forever –
a figure from a woodcut for a fable

designed to teach our children patience,
to show them what can be accomplished

over time – the thin limbs
stretching behind him in their thousands.

Hazel

Michael Longley

Not only has the hazel you gave me
Grown as high as our bedroom window,
It now canopies a helleborine,
A wild orchid as unexpected as
The pale yellow February catkins.

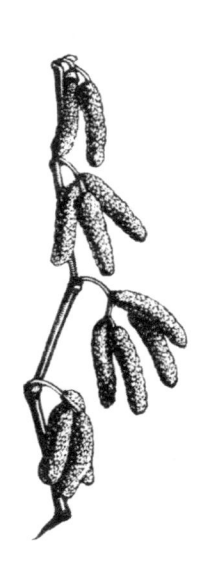

Planting the Alder
Seamus Heaney (1939-2013)

For the bark, dulled argent, roundly wrapped
And pigeon-collared.
For the splitter-splatter, guttering
Rain-flirt leaves.
For the snub and clot of the first green cones,
Smelted emerald, chlorophyll.
For the scut and scat of cones in winter,
So rattle-skinned, so fossil-brittle.
For the alder wood, flame-red when torn
Branch from branch.
But mostly for the swinging locks
Of yellow catkins.
Plant it, plant it,
Streel-head in the rain.

Leaf

for J.O. and L.O.
Alice Oswald

the leaf that now lies being made
in its shell of scale, the hush of things
unseen inside, the heartbeat of dead wood.
the slow through-flow that feeds
a form curled under, hour by hour
the thick reissuing starlike shapes
of cells and pores and water-rods
which builds up, which becomes a pressure,
a gradual fleshing out of a longing for light,
a small hand unfolding, feeling about.
into that hand the entire
object of the self being coldly placed,
the provisional, the inexplicable I
in mid-air, meeting the wind and dancing

The Trees

Philip Larkin (1922-1985)

The trees are coming into leaf
Like something almost being said;
The recent buds relax and spread,
Their greenness is a kind of grief.

Is it that they are born again
And we grow old? No, they die too,
Their yearly trick of looking new
Is written down in rings of grain.

Yet still the unresting castles thresh
In fullgrown thickness every May.
Last year is dead, they seem to say,
Begin afresh, afresh, afresh.

from **The Wood**

Charlotte Brontë (1816-1855)

But two miles more, and then we rest!
   Well, there is still an hour of day,
And long the brightness of the West
   Will light us on our devious way;
Sit then, awhile, here in this wood –
So total is the solitude,
   We safely may delay.

These massive roots afford a seat,
   Which seems for weary travellers made.
There rest. The air is soft and sweet
   In this sequestered forest glade,
And there are scents of flowers around,
The evening dew draws from the ground;
   How soothingly they spread!

Wood Not Yet Out

Alice Oswald

closed and containing everything, the land
leaning all round to block it from the wind,
a squirrel sprinting in startles and sees
sections of distance tilted through the trees
and where you jump the fence a flap of sacking
does for a stile, you walk through webs, the cracking
bushtwigs break their secrecies, the sun
vanishes up, instantly come and gone.
once in, you hardly notice as you move,
the wood keeps lifting up its hope, I love
to stand among the last trees listening down
to the releasing branches where I've been –
the rain, thinking I've gone, crackles the air
and calls by name the leaves that aren't yet there

Windfalls
Jon Stallworthy (1935-2014)

There are stars in the grass,
Orion behind
the apple tree. I'll find
a jam jar and a glass

and, kneeling in the dark
where amorous fireflies,
catching each other's eyes,
speak with a tender spark,

I'll fill an indoor sky
with fallen starlight –
enough, at least, to write
a love poem by.

Loveliest of Trees

A E Housman (1859-1936)

Loveliest of trees, the cherry now
Is hung with bloom along the bough,
And stands about the woodland ride
Wearing white for Eastertide.

Now, of my threescore years and ten,
Twenty will not come again,
And take from seventy springs a score,
It only leaves me fifty more.

And since to look at things in bloom
Fifty springs are little room,
About the woodlands I will go
To see the cherry hung with snow.

from **Orchard Idyll**
Sydney Matthewman (1902-1970)

The wind among the apple-trees
Is murmurous as distant seas,
And from my orchard-shaded house
I see the sea-green of the boughs
Break into crests of blossomy spray,
Where the adventurous bees all day
Ride on the surf, and butterflies
Spread fragile canvas to the skies,
Yacht-like to sail my orchard seas.
But soon the restless summer breeze
Spreads my foam-blossom far and wide
Confetti for a summer bride –
Yet sighs that spring so soon should pass
With the white petals on the grass.
Now a deeper peace comes over
Apple-trees and orchard clover;
Summer rests and drowsing there
Hushes the uneasy air.

May Rain
Kerry Hardie

It is May, and the rain is falling.
It's warm. Everything's swelling and drinking,
the birds have gone in, they cheep deep
in the walls of the white-thorn
that make of the garden a kingdom.

The whitethorn is flowering, it holds out its arms
to the rain. When the rain stops the perfume will rise,
a silence inside the green wall
that is splashed and dripping with blossom.
When the rain stops the birds will burst out,
will shout like the newly-arisen, up into the sky,
and the snails will go carrying their whorled shells about,
they'll vanish the shoots,
they'll pattern the new leaves with cut-work.

Me, too. I will come from the darkness
inside the green door, will walk the lost garden,
sniffing and touching,
sleeves wet, and the cuffs of my trousers,
hair wet from the pour of round drops
from the brushed-against leaves,
life wet from the green soak
of birdsong and roundness and rain.

Trees
Fleur Adcock

Elm, laburnum, hawthorn, oak:
all the incredible leaves expand
on their dusty branches, like
Japanese paper flowers in water,
like anything one hardly believes
will really work this time; and
I am a stupefied spectator
as usual. What are they all, these
multiverdant, variously-made
soft sudden things, these leaves?
So I walk solemnly in the park
with a copy of *Let's Look at Trees*
from the children's library,
identifying leaf-shapes and bark
while behind my back, at home,
my own garden is turning into a wood.
Before my house the pink may tree
lolls its heavy heads over mine
to grapple my hair as I come
in; at the back door I walk out
under lilac. The two elders
(I let them grow for the wine)
hang vastly over the fence, no doubt
infuriating my tidy neighbours.
In the centre the apple tree
needs pruning. And everywhere,
soaring over the garden shed,
camouflaged by roses, or snaking
up through the grass like vertical worms,
grows every size of sycamore.
Last year we attacked them; I saw
my son, so tender to ants, so sad

over dead caterpillars, hacking
at living roots as thick as his arms,
drenching the stumps with creosote.
No use: they continue to grow.
Under the grass, the ground
must be peppered with winged seeds,
meshed with a tough stringy net
of roots; and the house itself undermined
by wandering wood. Shall we see
the floorboards lifted one morning
by these indomitable weeds,
or find in the airing-cupboard
a rather pale sapling?
And if we do, will it be
worse than cracked pipes or dry rot?
Trees I can tolerate; they are why
I chose this house—for the apple tree,
elder, buddleia, lilac, may;
and outside my bedroom window, higher
every week, its leaves unfurling
pink at the twig-tips (composite
in form) the tallest sycamore.

Tree

Jane Hirshfield

It is foolish
to let a young redwood
grow next to a house.

Even in this
one lifetime,
you will have to choose.

That great calm being,
this clutter of soup pots and books –

Already the first branch-tips brush at the window.
Softly, calmly, immensity taps at your life.

To a Tree
Elizabeth Bishop (1911-1979)

Oh, tree outside my window, we are kin,
    For you ask nothing of a friend but this:
To lean against the window and peer in
    And watch me move about! Sufficient bliss

For me, who stand behind its framework stout,
    Full of my tiny tragedies and grotesque grieves,
To lean against the window and peer out,
    Admiring infinites'mal leaves.

Winter Plums

Clive James

Two winter plum trees grow beside my door.
Throughout the cold months they had little pink
Flowers all over them as if they wore
Nightdresses, and their branches, black as ink
By sunset, looked as if a Japanese
Painter, while painting air, had painted these

Two winter plum trees. Summer now at last
Has warmed their leaves and all the blooms are gone.
A year that I might not have had has passed.
Bare branches are my signal to go on,
But soon the brave flowers of the winter plums
Will flare again, and I must take what comes.

Two winter plum trees that will outlive me.
Thriving with colour even in the snow,
They'll snatch a triumph from adversity.
All right for them, but can the same be so
For someone who, seeing their buds remade
From nothing, will be less pleased than afraid?

Wild Plums
Gillian Clarke

The old trees lean together
one in the arms of the other,
mossed, wind-broken, snag-branched,
seeded a century back by chance.

Our first spring – remember? –
starbursts of petals
from stubborn wood that April,
and every September

sweet nameless plums
to pick from the air as we pass.
At night fruit thudding in grass
is the drumbeat of dreams.

Blue-skinned, gold-fleshed,
simmered and stored in sugar and spice
till a time of thaw, prunus fresh
on the tongue, a tingle of ice.

Into the Trees
Ruth Gilbert (1917-2016)

Fern-shadows, and the tall magnolia flowers
Drenching the air with perfume and with light,
This is the chosen, the appointed night
The shining instant in your Book of Hours.

You stand a moment listening to the bees
Recite some ancient rune, some ageless charm,
Then, light bow swinging, fiddle under arm
You walk into the silence of the trees.

Trees in the Garden

D H Lawrence (1885-1930)

Ah in the thunder air
how still the trees are!

And the lime-tree, lovely and tall, every leaf silent
hardly looses even a last breath of perfume.

And the ghostly, creamy coloured little tree of leaves
white, ivory white among the rambling greens
how evanescent, variegated elder, she hesitates on the green grass
as if, in another moment, she would disappear
with all her grace of foam!

And the larch that is only a column, it goes up too tall to see:
and the balsam-pines that are blue with the grey-blue blueness of
things from the sea,
and the young copper beech, its leaves red-rosy at the ends
how still they are together, they stand so still
in the thunder air, all strangers to one another
as the green grass glows upwards, strangers in the silent garden.

The Shadow Tree
Ilo Orleans (1897-1962)

I'd love to sit
   On the highest branch
But it's much too high
   For me;

So I sit on the grass
   Where the shadow falls,
On the top of
   The shadow tree.

Tree Climbing
Paul Batchelor

Grasp this: it doesn't matter if the rasp
of bark to palm is second nature or
if this is your first time, there are

no experts: ash or oak, the look of bole
or canopy means nothing till you throw
yourself off balance, wrap

your feet around the branch you hold
and from that new perspective see
how the world hangs: head over heels

it all floods back to a heart
that won't forget vertigo's bloodrush
nor come down when they call.

The plum tree
Helen Dunmore (1952-2017)

The plum was my parents' tree,
above them
as I was at my bedroom window
wondering why they chose to walk this way quietly
under the plum tree.

My sisters and I stopped playing
as they reached up and felt for the fruit.
It lay among bunches of leaves,
oval and oozing resin
out into pearls of gum.
They bit into the plums
without once glancing
back at the house.

Some years were thin:
white mildew streaking the trunk,
fruit buckled and green,

but one April
the tree broke from its temperate blossoming
and by late summer the branches
trailed earth, heavy with pound
after pound of bursting Victorias,

and I remember the oblivious steps
my parents took as they went quietly
out of the house one summer evening
to stand under the plum tree.

Coming Home at Twilight in Late Summer

Jane Kenyon (1947-1995)

We turned into the drive,
and gravel flew up from the tires
like sparks from a fire. So much
to be done – the unpacking, the mail
and papers ... the grass needed mowing ...
We climbed stiffly out of the car.
The shut-off engine ticked as it cooled.

And then we noticed the pear tree,
the limbs so heavy with fruit
they nearly touched the ground.
We went out to the meadow; our steps
made black holes in the grass;
and we each took a pear,
and ate, and were grateful.

A mortgage on a pear tree

Helen Dunmore (1952-2017)

A pear tree stands in its own maze.
It does not close its blossom all night
but holds out branchfuls of cool
wide-open flowers. Its slim leaves look black
and stir like tongues in the lamp-light.

It was here before the houses were built.
The owner grew wasteland and waited for values to rise.
The builders swerved a boundary sideways
to cup the tree in a garden. When they piled rubble
it was a soft cairn mounting the bole.

The first owner of the raw garden
came out and walked on the clay clods.
There was the pear tree, bent down
with small blunt fruits, each wide where the flower was,
shaped like a medlar, but sweet.

The ground was dense with fermenting pears,
half trodden to pulp, half eaten.
She could not walk without slipping.

Slowly she walked in her own maze,
sleepy, feeling the blood seep
down her cold fingers, down the spread branch
of veins which trails to the heart,

and remembered how she'd stood under a tree
holding out arms, with two school-friends.
It was the fainting-game,
played in the dinner-hour from pure boredom,
never recalled since. For years this was growing

to meet her, and now she's signed for her own
long mortgage over the pear tree
and is the gainer of its accrued beauty,

but when she goes into her bedroom
and draws her curtains against a spring night
the pear tree does not close its white blossom.
The flowers stay open with slim leaves flickering around them:
touched and used, they bear fruit.

Daphne with her Thighs in Bark
Eavan Boland

'Daphne with her thighs in bark
stretches towards me her leafy hands, ...
from Hugh Selwyn Mauberley Part 1, Section xii by Ezra Pound
(1920)

I have written this
so that,
in the next myth
my sister
will be wiser.

Let her learn from me:
the opposite of passion
is not virtue
but routine.

Look at me.
I can be cooking,
making coffee,
scrubbing wood perhaps,
and back it comes:
the crystalline,
the otherwhere,
the wood

where I was
when he began the chase.
And how I ran from him!

Pan-thighed
satyr-faced he was.

The trees reached out to me,
I silvered
and I quivered.
I shook out my foil of quick leaves
He snouted past.
What a fool I was!

I shall be here forever,
setting out the tea,
among the paunched copper
and the branching alloys,
the tin shine
of this kitchen
and the pine table.

Save face sister.
Fall. Stumble.
Rut with him.
His rough heat
will keep you warm.

You will be better off
than me
with your memories
down the garden
at the start of March,
unable to keep your eyes
off the chestnut tree –

just the way
it thrusts and hardens.

The Shepherd's Tree

John Clare (1793-1864)

Huge elm, with rifted trunk all notched and scarred,
Like to a warrior's destiny! I love
To stretch me often on thy shadowed sward,
And hear the laugh of summer leaves above;
Or on thy buttressed roots to sit, and lean
In careless attitude, and there reflect
On times and deeds and darings that have been –
Old castaways, now swallowed in neglect, –
While thou art towering in thy strength of heart,
Stirring the soul to vain imaginings
In which life's sordid being hath no part.
The wind of that eternal ditty sings,
Humming of future things, that burn the mind
To leave some fragment of itself behind.

from Eclogue I
Virgil

Translated by H R Fairclough (1862-1938)

Meliboeus
[1] You, Tityrus, lie under the canopy of a slender beech, wooing the woodland Muse on slender reed, but we are leaving our country's bounds and sweet fields. We are outcasts from our country; you, Tityrus, at ease beneath the shade, teach the woods to re-echo 'fair Amaryllis'.

The Beech Tree

Michael Longley

Leaning back like a lover against this beech tree's
Two-hundred-year-old pewter trunk, I look up
Through skylights into the leafy cumulus, and join
Everybody who has teetered where these huge roots
Spread far and wide our motionless mossy dance,
As though I'd begun my eclogues with a beech
As Virgil does, the brown envelopes unfolding
Like fans their transparent downy leaves, tassels
And prickly cups, mast, a fall of vermilion
And copper and gold, then room in the branches
For the full moon and her dusty lakes, winter
And the poet who recollects his younger self
And improvises a last line for the georgics
About snoozing under this beech tree's canopy.

The Oak Wood
for Stephen Warburton (1950-2004)
Gillian Clarke

Stephen, your paper slips still mark the page
in the *Cardiganshire County History*
where you noted the pollen evidence of beech
in the ancient forest, four thousand years ago.

Whenever we're out late in the wood in summer
waiting for badgers, pretending to be trees,
and the rooks come home to roost, so quiet,
one by one folding their wings like shadows,

and when we stand to go, too cold to wait,
and the whole wood breaks out in a great commotion
of woken night birds, or when we walk in the ruins
of blue, the stalks and seedheads of bluebells

turning to death and resurrection in one moment,
when the wood is holy ground dreaming cathedrals
in its columns and arcades, or when leaves turn,
and owls cry in the lofty clerestories,

you'll be there with your good counsel,
your name spoken, and on the path, your footfall.

Not Dead

Robert Graves (1895-1985)

Walking through trees to cool my heat and pain,
I know that David's with me here again.
All that is simple, happy, strong, he is.
Caressingly I stroke
Rough bark of the friendly oak.
A brook goes bubbling by: the voice is his.
Turf burns with pleasant smoke;
I laugh at chaffinch and at primroses.
All that is simple, happy, strong, he is.
Over the whole wood in a little while
Breaks his slow smile.

The English Elms
Carol Ann Duffy

Seven Sisters in Tottenham,
long gone, except for their names,
were English elms.

Others stood at the edge of farms,
twinned with the shapes of clouds
like green rhymes;
or cupped the beads of the rain
in their leaf palms;
or glowered, grim giants, warning of storms.

In the hedgerows in old films,
elegiacally, they loom,
the English elms;
or find posthumous fame
in the lines of poems –
the music making elm –
for ours is a world without them ...

to whom the artists came,
time upon time,
scumbling, paint on their fingers and thumbs;
and the woodcutters, who knew the elm
was a coffin's deadly aim;
and the mavis, her filled nest unharmed
in the crook of a living, wooden arm;
and boys, with ball, bat, stumps
for a game;
and nursing ewes and lambs, calm
under English elms ...

great, masterpiece trees
who were overwhelmed.

What Kind of Times are These
Adrienne Rich (1929-2012)

There's a place between two stands of trees where the grass grows
      uphill
and the old revolutionary road breaks off into shadows
near a meeting-house abandoned by the persecuted
who disappeared into those shadows.

I've walked there picking mushrooms at the edge of dread, but
      don't be fooled,
this isn't a Russian poem, this is not somewhere else but here,
our country moving closer to its own truth and dread,
its own ways of making people disappear.

I won't tell you where the place is, the dark mesh of the woods
meeting the unmarked strip of light—
ghost-ridden crossroads, leafmold paradise:
I know already who wants to buy it, sell it, make it disappear.

And I won't tell you where it is, so why do I tell you
anything? Because you still listen, because in times like these
to have you listen at all, it's necessary
to talk about trees.

Two Trees

Don Paterson

One morning, Don Miguel got out of bed
with one idea rooted in his head:
to graft his orange to his lemon tree.
It took him the whole day to work them free,
lay open their sides, and lash them tight.
For twelve months, from the shame or from the fright
they put forth nothing; but one day there appeared
two lights in the dark leaves. Over the years
the limbs would get themselves so tangled up
each bough looked like it gave a double crop,
and not one kid in the village didn't know
the magic tree in Miguel's patio.

The man who bought the house had had no dream
so who can say what dark malicious whim
led him to take his axe and split the bole
along its fused seam, then dig two holes.
And no, they did not die from solitude;
nor did their branches bear a sterile fruit;
nor did their unhealed flanks weep every spring
for those four yards that lost them everything,
as each strained on its shackled root to face
the other's empty, intricate embrace.
They were trees, and trees don't weep or ache or shout.
And trees are all this poem is about.

The Sycamore
for Henry Caudill
Wendell Berry

In the place that is my own place, whose earth
I am shaped in and must bear, there is an old tree growing,
a great sycamore that is a wondrous healer of itself.
Fences have been tied to it, nails driven into it,
hacks and whittles cut in it, the lightning has burned it.
There is no year it has flourished in
that has not harmed it. There is a hollow in it
that is its death, though its living brims whitely
at the lip of the darkness and flows outward.
Over all its scars has come the seamless white
of the bark. It bears the gnarls of its history
healed over. It has risen to a strange perfection
in the warp and bending of its long growth.
It has gathered all accidents into its purpose.
It has become the intention and radiance of its dark fate.
It is a fact, sublime, mystical and unassailable.
In all the country there is no other like it.
I recognize in it a principle, an indwelling
the same as itself, and greater, that I would be ruled by.
I see that it stands in its place, and feeds upon it,
and is fed upon, and is native, and maker.

The Hollow Tree
John Clare (1793-1864)

How oft a summer shower hath started me
To seek for shelter in an hollow tree:
Old huge ash-dotterel wasted to a shell,
Whose vigorous head still grew and flourished well,
Where ten might sit upon the battered floor
And still look round discovering room for more,
And he who chose a hermit life to share
Might have a door and make a cabin there –
They seemed so like a house that our desires
Would call them so and make our gypsy fires
And eat field dinners of the juicy peas
Till we were wet and drabbled to the knees.
But in our old tree house, rain as it might,
Not one drop fell although it rained till night.

Wealth in Difference
Harriet Fraser

from specksmall seeds
these woods have grown
and tower now, witness
to the exhalations of earth
and leaf-brushed air

to walk here is to be woven in
with season's change
mist, sun, rain
all around us life

this ancestry of veterans
makes a library of place
textured life in trunk and branch

    pause: count the wealth
    in the difference of trees

oak, ash, birch, twisted hawthorn
hazel, sycamore, larch
each tree rooted deep

we are layered in with greens
and the writing of wind
on the black lake

above it all: the pine
rising

The Way through the Woods
Rudyard Kipling (1865-1936)

They shut the road through the woods
Seventy years ago.
Weather and rain have undone it again,
And now you would never know
There was once a road through the woods
Before they planted the trees.
It is underneath the coppice and heath,
And the thin anemones.
Only the keeper sees
That, where the ring-dove broods,
And the badgers roll at ease,
There was once a road through the woods.
Yet, if you enter the woods
Of a summer evening late,
When the night-air cools on the trout-ringed pools
Where the otter whistles his mate,
(They fear not men in the woods,
Because they see so few.)
You will hear the beat of a horse's feet,
And the swish of a skirt in the dew,
Steadily cantering through
The misty solitudes,
As though they perfectly knew
The old lost road through the woods.
But there is no road through the woods.

Lawmarnock Wood in Autumn

Jim Carruth

You, who never asked for anything
now and again would mention
how much you loved
that view across the valley,
We talked of photographs,
paintings – framed gift for you.

Now it's too late to capture
what you loved most,
the wood's slow turning,
those moments before leaf fall,
the way it lifts clear of early mist
from the banks of the Locher burn
to hug the contours of two hills.

The skyline of your working days, a vocal
tapestry of russets and yellows,
a gathering of old friends after the harvest.
You'd watch and listen
to the sway of their dancing
as the last of the berries
were picked from the hedgerows.

Scents of change
in a strengthening breeze, in the stiff
ache of your joints;
that growing taste of damp
you treasured for its burnished afterglow,
offering up both bird chorus and lonely owl,
celebration and melancholy.

Mother, this is January.
I cannot give you again
Lawmarnock Wood in Autumn.

The Apple Orchard

Rainer Maria Rilke (1875-1926)

Come let us watch the sun go down
and walk in twilight through the orchard's green.
Does it not seem as if we had for long
collected, saved and harboured within us
old memories? To find releases and seek
new hopes, remembering half-forgotten joys,
mingled with darkness coming from within,
as we randomly voice our thoughts aloud
wandering beneath these harvest-laden trees
reminiscent of Dürer woodcuts, branches
which, bent under the fully ripened fruit,
wait patiently, trying to outlast, to
serve another season's hundred days of toil,
straining, uncomplaining, by not breaking
but succeeding, even though the burden
should at times seem almost past endurance.
Not to falter! Not to be found wanting!

Thus must it be, when willingly you strive
throughout a long and uncomplaining life,
committed to one goal: to give yourself!
And silently to grow and to bear fruit.

Apple Country
Alison Brackenbury

I am living, quite unplanned, by apple country.
Worcesters come the earliest: sea green
with darkest red, even the flesh, veined pink.
They have a bloom no hand can brush away
sweet breath made visible. But do not think
to have them through the dark days: they'll not keep,
for that choose Coxes flecked with gold
which wrinkle into kindness, winter's fires.

Where I was born they let no flowering trees
in the bare fields, which grow my dreams, which hold
only the lasting crops, potato, wheat.
How low the houses crouch upon their soil
with fruitless hedges; at the barn's end, cars:

none yours. I have no art for probing back
to such dark roots. Yet if you pass this place
though skies shine lean with frost, no softness dapples
white wall to cave of leaf, yet stranger, knock.

                For I will give you apples.

from **Leaf-fall**
(for Séan)
Kerry Hardie

'Chestnuts are the stubbornest.'
The pithy brown husks
that shielded the fruits
lie scattered about on the grass.
Also leaves.
But so many still on the trees.

'It takes a frost.
Don't you remember?'

Yes, he remembers.
The first bitter night
and the leaves all unhook.
They drift in the stillness,
they settle like moths on the grass.

He likes these hidden patterns and decisions:
trees, opening their hands in the night,
letting fall
what they have no more use for;
like cycles, secrets, metaphysics.

Leaves
Choman Hardi

Can you see the leaves, each fresh and lively
shivering on their stems? Do you notice
how they turn left, right, left again?
Like a synchronised army of soldiers
they sway, sending waves up the height of the tree.

Have you noticed how the branch tips
are lost in greenness, up there, where the broody rook
has laid her eggs? In autumn the trees go blonde,
so delicate that a mild wind can undress them.
How graciously they fall, following each other,
piling up, crunchy under our feet.

Whitebeam

Paul Farley

The sixty-miles-per-hour plants, the growth
that lines the summer corridors of sight
along our major roads, the overlooked
backdrop to Preston 37 miles.
Speed camera foliage; the white flowers
of Mays and Junes, the scarlet fruits of autumn
lay wasted in the getting from A to B.
Hymn to forward-thinking and planting schemes,
though some seem in two minds: the greenwood leaves
are white-furred, have a downy underside
as if the heartwood knew in its heart of hearts
the days among beech and oak would lead to these
single file times, these hard postings
and civilised itself with handkerchiefs.

The Future of Forestry

C S Lewis (1898–1963)

How will the legend of the age of trees
Feel, when the last tree falls in England?
When the concrete spreads and the town conquers
The country's heart; when contraceptive
Tarmac's laid where farm has faded,
Tramline flows where slept a hamlet,
And shop-fronts, blazing without a stop from
Dover to Wrath, have glazed us over?
Simplest tales will then bewilder
The questioning children, "What was a chestnut?
Say what it means to climb a Beanstalk,
Tell me, grandfather, what an elm is.
What was Autumn? They never taught us."
Then, told by teachers how once from mould
Came growing creatures of lower nature
Able to live and die, though neither
Beast nor man, and around them wreathing
Excellent clothing, breathing sunlight –
Half understanding, their ill-acquainted
Fancy will tint their wonder-paintings
Trees as men walking, wood-romances
Of goblins stalking in silky green,
Of milk-sheen froth upon the lace of hawthorn's
Collar, pallor in the face of birchgirl.
So shall a homeless time, though dimly
Catch from afar (for soul is watchfull)
A sight of tree-delighted Eden.

The Poplar

Seamus Heaney (1939-2013)

Wind shakes the big poplar, quicksilvering
The whole tree in a single sweep.
What bright scale fell and left this needle quivering?
What loaded balances have come to grief?

Binsey Poplars
felled 1879

Gerard Manley Hopkins (1844-1889)

My aspens dear, whose airy cages quelled,
Quelled or quenched in leaves the leaping sun,
All felled, felled, are all felled;
   Of a fresh and following folded rank
        Not spared, not one
          That dandled a sandalled
           Shadow that swam or sank
On meadow and river and wind-wandering weed-winding bank.

O if we but knew what we do
      When we delve or hew —
   Hack and rack the growing green!
      Since country is so tender
  To touch, her being só slender,
  That, like this sleek and seeing ball
  But a prick will make no eye at all,

Where we, even where we mean
     To mend her we end her,
    When we hew or delve:
After-comers cannot guess the beauty been.
   Ten or twelve, only ten or twelve
     Strokes of havoc únselve
       The sweet especial scene,
   Rural scene, a rural scene,
   Sweet especial rural scene.

Given: A Log of Wood; Make: A Fiddle
Ruth Gilbert (1917-2016)

A block of Maple, seasoned from a tree
Fifty years growing, brought from Italy.
You smile, recalling warm Italian skies,
A dream of far Cremona in your eyes.
'Mere wood!' we say. 'Mere wood!' you say again
Then lean your hand upon the faultless grain
Exultingly; 'Wood, Palette, Words, or Clay,
Each shapes his music in a different way
And of that substance known and loved the best.
My choice lies here; what sculptor's fingers rest
Who sees his marble mute and beckoning?
Give me my tools, and wood, mere wood shall sing!'

Prayer of the Woods

Anon

I am the heat of your hearth on the cold winter nights, the friendly shade screening you from the summer sun, and my fruits are refreshing draughts quenching your thirst as you journey on.

I am the beam that holds your house, the board of your table, the bed on which you lie, and the timber that builds your boat.

I am the handle of your hoe, the door of your homestead, the wood of your cradle, and the shell of your coffin.

I am the bread of kindness and the flower of beauty. Ye who pass by, listen to my prayer: Harm me not.

The first version of this well-known verse can be traced back to a poem written in 1914 by the Portuguese writer Alberto de Veiga Simões.

Winter Trees
William Carlos Williams (1883-1963)

All the complicated details
of the attiring and
the disattiring are completed!
A liquid moon
moves gently among
the long branches.
Thus having prepared their buds
against a sure winter
the wise trees
stand sleeping in the cold.

A Black Birch in Winter

Richard Wilbur (1921-2017)

You might not know this old tree by its bark,
Which once was striate, smooth, and glossy-dark,
So deep now are the rifts which separate
Its roughened surface into flake and plate.
Fancy might less remind you of a birch
Than of mosaic columns in a church
Like Ara Coeli or the Lateran,
Or the trenched features of an agèd man.
Still, do not be too much persuaded by
These knotty furrows and these tesserae
To think of patterns made from outside-in
Or finished wisdom in a shriveled skin.
Old trees are doomed to annual rebirth,
New wood, new life, new compass, greater girth,
And this is all their wisdom and their art—
To grow, stretch, crack, and not yet come apart.

Haiku: Willows
Wendy Cope

Willows white with frost:
like fireworks that whooshed, sparkled
and froze in the air.

Pruning in Frost
Alice Oswald

Last night, without a sound,
a ghost of a world lay down on a world,

trees like dream-wrecks
coralled with increments of frost.

Found crevices
and wound and wound
the clock-spring cobwebs.

All life's ribbon frozen mid-fling.

Oh I am
stone thumbs,
feet of glass.

Work knocks in me the winter's nail.

I can imagine
Pain, turned heron,
could fly off slowly in a creak of wings.

And I'd be staring, like one of those
cold-holy and granite kings,
getting carved into this effigy of orchard.

In the Dark Pine-wood

James Joyce (1882-1941)

In the dark pine-wood
I would we lay,
In deep cool shadow
At noon of day.

How sweet to lie there,
Sweet to kiss,
Where the great pine-forest
Enaisled is!

Thy kiss descending
Sweeter were
With a soft tumult
Of thy hair.

O unto the pine-wood
At noon of day
Come with me now,
Sweet love, away.

Pine Trees and the Sky: Evening
Rupert Brooke (1887-1915)

I'd watched the sorrows of the evening sky,
And smelt the sea, and earth, and the warm clover,
And heard the waves, and the seagull's mocking cry.

And in them all was only the old cry,
That song they always sing – 'The best is over!
You may remember now, and think, and sigh,
O silly lover!'
And I was tired and sick that all was over,
And because I,
For all my thinking, never could recover
One moment of the good hours that were over.
And I was sorry and sick, and wished to die.

Then from the sad west turning wearily,
I saw the pines against the white north sky,
Very beautiful, and still, and bending over
Their sharp black heads against a quiet sky.
And there was peace in them; and I
Was happy, and forgot to play the lover,
And laughed, and did no longer wish to die;
Being glad of you, O pine-trees and the sky!

See yonder leafless trees

Ralph Waldo Emerson (1803-1882)

See yonder leafless trees against the sky,
How they diffuse themselves into the air,
And ever subdividing separate,
Limbs into branches, branches into twigs.
As if they loved the element, and hasted
To dissipate their being into it.

Those Trees
Ruth Fainlight

It must be the dawn chorus –
or are the birds that just woke me
perched on those trees:
my lost garden burgeoning beyond
the window, years receding
like scrims of painted scenery,
flimsy curtains drawn across
and closing off the street outside?

Those trees, here, are fuller
and taller than they were there and then.
Their branches are thicker, reach further now –
changed by how many years' growth?
Some part of my being stayed
with them, witnessing time
alter the shapes
of bushes and hedges, adding, subtracting,
substance and meaning. Are real birds
really singing this early, this winter
city morning – a dawn chorus –
or am I in that other house?
For they are more immediate
than memory: those trees.

little tree

e e cummings (1894-1962)

little tree
little silent Christmas tree
you are so little
you are more like a flower

who found you in the green forest
and were you very sorry to come away?
see   i will comfort you
because you smell so sweetly

i will kiss your cool bark
and hug you safe and tight
just as your mother would,
only don't be afraid

look   the spangles
that sleep all the year in a dark box
dreaming of being taken out and allowed to shine,
the balls the chains red and gold the fluffy threads,

put up your little arms
and i'll give them all to you to hold
every finger shall have its ring
and there won't be a single place dark or unhappy

then when you're quite dressed
you'll stand in the window for everyone to see
and how they'll stare!
oh but you'll be very proud

and my little sister and i will take hands
and looking up at our beautiful tree
we'll dance and sing
'Noel Noel'

The Tree
Wendy Cope

We had to leave our home. We travelled here
With all our worldly goods – box after box
Of crockery and books, our furniture,
Our pictures, mirrors, lamps and rugs and clocks.
In its pot our precious Christmas tree,
A straggly, adolescent, four years old,
Survived the journey, waited patiently
Till it was time to come in from the cold.
Now it's lit up in all its annual glory,
Hung with treasures taken out of store.
Every little trinket tells a story,
A memoir of the life we had before.
We got through the disruption and the pain.
The tree is telling us we're home again.

The Firewood Poem
Celia Congreve

Beechwood fires are bright and clear
If the logs are kept a year,
Chestnut's only good they say,
If for logs 'tis laid away.
Make a fire of Elder tree,
Death within your house will be;
But ash new or ash old,
Is fit for a queen with crown of gold.

Birch and fir logs burn too fast
Blaze up bright and do not last,
It is by the Irish said
Hawthorn bakes the sweetest bread.
Elm wood burns like churchyard mould,
E'en the very flames are cold
But ash green or ash brown
Is fit for a queen with golden crown.

Poplar gives a bitter smoke,
Fills your eyes and makes you choke,
Apple wood will scent your room
Pear wood smells like flowers in bloom
Oaken logs, if dry and old
Keep away the winter's cold
But ash wet or ash dry
a king shall warm his slippers by.

The firewood poem is believed to be first published in THE TIMES newspaper on March 2nd 1930

Mr Pollard
Roger McGough

In the dead of last night
we had a visit from Mr Pollard.
With his giant scissors
he lopped off the branches
from the trees in our road.

Today, like teenagers with bad haircuts,
they stand, gawky and embarrassed.
Birds stay clear. The sun bides its time.

The Oak Tree
Matsuo Basho (1644-1694)

The oak tree:
not interested
in cherry blossoms.

With People, So With Trees
Mervyn Peake (1911-1968)

With people, so with trees: where there are groups
Of either, men or trees, some will remain
Aloof while others cluster where one stoops
To breathe some dusky secret. Some complain

And some gesticulate and some are blind;
Some toss their heads above green towns; some freeze
For lack of love in copses of mankind;
Some laugh; some mourn; with people, so with trees.

Acknowledgements

We would like to thank Neil Morgan for his help and support in publishing this collection.

We would also like to thank the following artists and poets for permission to publish their work: Carry Akroyd, Jonathan Ashworth (www.jonathanashworth.com), Sue Butler, Jim Carruth, Camilla Charnock, Harriet Fraser (www.somewhere-nowhere.com), Jonathan Gibbs *Tree at my Window* 100 x 80 mm (www.jonathangibbs.com), Michael S Glaser, John F Greenwood (Museums & Galleries, City of Bradford MDC), Anne Hayward, Jane Hirshfield, Anita Klein, Kay Leverton, Miriam Macgregor, Sue Scullard, Richard Wagener.

We gratefully acknowledge permission to reprint copyright material in this book as follows:
Trees from *Poems (1960-2000)* by Fleur Adcock (Bloodaxe Books, 2000); *Tree Climbing* from *The Sinking Road* by Paul Batchelor (Bloodaxe Books, 2008); *Look it Over* and *The Sycamore* by Wendell Berry Copyright © 2012 by Wendell Berry. Reprinted by permission of Counterpoint Press; *To a Tree* from *Complete Poems* by Elizabeth Bishop Published by Jonathan Cape Reprinted by permission of The Random House Group Ltd © 1983; *Daphne with her Thighs in Bark* from *New Selected Poems* by Eavan Boland (Carcanet Press Ltd); *Apple Country* from *Selected Poems* by Alison Brackenbury (Carcanet Press Ltd); *Wild Plums* from *Ice* by Gillian Clarke (Carcanet Press Ltd); *The Oak Wood* from *Recipe for Water* by Gillian Clarke (Carcanet Press Ltd); *The Tree* and *Haiku: Willows* from *Anecdotal Evidence* by Wendy Cope (Faber and Faber Ltd); *Quercus, oak* by Alexander Cozens © The Trustees of the Natural History Museum, London; *The English Elms* from *The Bees* by Carol Ann Duffy. Published by Macmillan Publishers Ltd, 2011. Copyright © Carol Ann Duffy. Reproduced by permission of the author c/o Rogers, Coleridge & White Ltd, 20 Powis Mews, London W11 1JN; *The plum tree* and *A mortgage on a pear tree* from *Out of the Blue: Poems 1974-2001* by Helen Dunmore (Bloodaxe Books, 2001); *Those Trees* from *New and Collected Poems* by Ruth Fainlight (Bloodaxe Books, 2010); *Whitebeam* from *Tramp in Flames* by Paul Farley published by Picador © 2006 Reproduced with permission of the Licensor through Plsclear; *Not Dead* from *Complete Poems in One Volume* by Robert Graves (Carcanet Press Ltd); *Into the Trees* and *Given: A Log of Wood; Make: A Fiddle* by Ruth Gilbert, with permission from the poet's daughter Pippa Mackay; *Leaves* from *Considering the Women* by Choman Hardi (Bloodaxe Books, 2015); *May Rain* and *Leaf-fall (for Séan)* extract, from *The Zebra Stood in the Night* by Kerry Hardie (Bloodaxe Books, 2014); *Planting the Alder* from *District and Circle* by Seamus Heaney (Faber and Faber Ltd); *The Poplar* from *The Spirit Level* by Seamus Heaney (Faber and Faber Ltd); *Tree* from *Each Happiness Ringed by Lions: Selected Poems* by Jane Hirshfield (Bloodaxe Books, 2006); *Winter Plums* from *Sentenced to Life* by Clive James published by Picador (2016) Reproduced with permission of the Licensor through Plsclear; *Coming Home at Twilight in Late Summer* from *Collected Poems* by Jane Kenyon. Copyright © 2005 by The Estate of Jane Kenyon. Reprinted with the permission of The Permissions Company, Inc on behalf of Graywolf Press, www.graywolfpress.org; *The Trees* from *Collected Poems* by Philip Larkin (Faber and Faber Ltd); *Warm Weather Coming* and *Hazel Catkins* from *Four Hedges* by Clare Leighton 1935 © The Estate of Clare Leighton; *The Future of Forestry* by C S Lewis © C S Lewis Pte Ltd. Reprinted by permission; *Hazel* from *Angel Hill* by Michael Longley Published by Jonathan Cape Reprinted by permission of The Random House Group Ltd © 2017; *The Beech Tree* from *The Weather in Japan* by Michael Longley Published by Jonathan Cape Reprinted by permission of The Random House Group Ltd © 2000; *Mr Pollard* by Roger McGough from *Poetry Pie* © Roger McGough, 2015) is printed by permission of United Agents (www.unitedagents.co.uk) on behalf of Roger McGough; *Rosy Red Apples* Lino cut © Clare Melinsky; *Planting* from *The Wound Register* by Esther Morgan (Bloodaxe Books, 2018); *The Shadow Tree* by Ilo Orleans, reprinted by permission of Karen S Solomon; *Woods etc.*, *Wood Not Yet Out, Leaf for J.O. and L.O.* from *Woods etc.* by Alice Oswald (Faber and Faber Ltd); *Pruning in Frost* from *The Thing in the Gap Stone Stile* by Alice Oswald (Faber and Faber Ltd); *Two Trees* from *Rain* by Don Paterson. Published by Faber and Faber, 2009. Copyright © Don Paterson. Reproduced by permission of the author c/o Rogers, Coleridge & White Ltd, 20 Powis Mews, London W11 1JN; *With People, So With Trees* by Mervyn Peake © Estate of Mervyn Peake. Reproduced by permission of the British Library; *Edge of the Woods* and *Downs in Winter* by Howard Phipps, by permission of the artist; *What Kind of Times Are These*, Copyright © 2016 by the Adrienne Rich Literary Trust. Copyright © 1995 by Adrienne Rich, from *Collected Poems: 1950-2012* by Adrienne Rich. Used by permission of W W Norton & Company Inc; *The Poet Tree* by Michael Shepherd © Michael Shepherd reproduced with permission from his publishers Godstow Press; *Windfalls* from *The Anzac Sonata: New and Selected Poems* by Jon Stallworthy ©1986 published by W W Norton & Company Inc, reprinted with permission from the poet's family; Two images by Reynolds Stone © Reynolds Stone Estate; *A Black Birch in Winter* reprinted from Richard Wilbur's *Collected Poems 1943-2004 (2005)*, courtesy of The Waywiser Press (waywiser-press.com); *Winter Trees* from *Collected Poems Vol 1 1909-1939* by William Carlos Williams (Carcanet Press Ltd).
All Bloodaxe poems are reproduced with permission of Bloodaxe Books on behalf of the author www.bloodaxebooks.com

Every effort has been made to trace or contact all copyright holders. The publishers would be pleased to rectify any omissions brought to their notice at the earliest opportunity.

The Poet Tree
Michael Shepherd (1929-2010)

Tenderly
with its soft leaves
the tree shaded the poet
as he wrote

and as its leaves fell
and the year turned
the tree wished
that it might be reborn
as a book of poems

and so it was

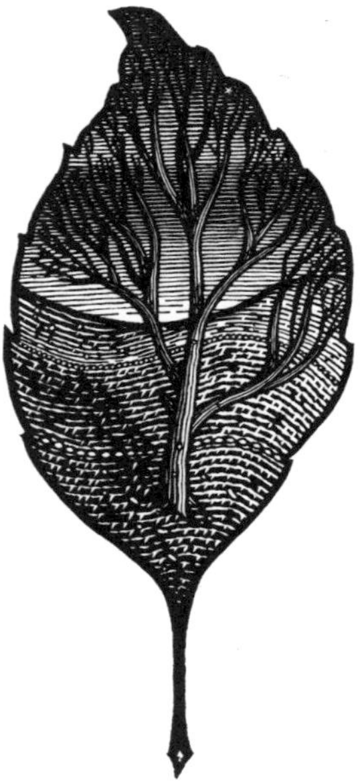